What Good Is an I?

amicus readers

1

by Marie Powell

amicus readers

Say Hello to Amicus Readers.

You'll find our helpful dog, Amicus, chasing a ball—to let you know the reading level of a book.

1

Learn to Read

Frequent repetition, high frequency words, and close photo-text matches introduce familiar topics and provide ample support for brand new readers.

2

Read Independently

Some repetition is mixed with varied sentence structures and a select amount of new vocabulary words are introduced with text and photo support.

3

Read to Know More

Interesting facts and engaging art and photos give fluent readers fun books both for reading practice and to learn about new topics.

Amicus Readers are published by Amicus
P.O. Box 1329, Mankato, MN 56002
www.amicuspublishing.us

Library of Congress Cataloging-in-Publication Data

Powell, Marie, 1958-
   What good is an I? / by Marie Powell.
      pages cm. -- (Vowels)
   Summary: "Beginning readers are introduced to the vowel I and its sounds and uses."-- Provided by publisher.
   ISBN 978-1-60753-710-6 (library binding)
   ISBN 978-1-60753-814-1 (ebook)
   1. Vowels--Juvenile literature. 2. English language--Vowels--Juvenile literature. I. Title.
   PE1157.P6943 2015
   428.1'3--dc23
                2014045794

Photo Credits: iStockphoto, cover; Valentyn Volkov/Shutterstock Images, 1; Shutterstock Images, 3, 8, 11, 12-13, 14-15, 16 (bottom left); Bowden Images/iStockphoto, 5; Creativa Images/Shutterstock Images, 6-7, 16 (bottom right); iStock/Thinkstock, 16 (top left); Lori Sparkia/Shutterstock Images, 16 (top right)

Produced for Amicus by The Peterson Publishing Company and Red Line Editorial.

Editor Jenna Gleisner
Designer Craig Hinton

Printed in Malaysia
10 9 8 7 6 5 4 3 2 1

What good is an **I**? **I** is a vowel, like A, E, O, U, and Y. What sound does **I** make?

I can have a long sound, like its name. Mike will ride his bike to the store.

I can have a short sound.
Nick will walk with his
little sister.

I can start a word. Ivy reaches into the icy cold freezer.

I can come in the middle of a word. Tim licks his cone before it drips on his shirt.

I can come at the end of a word. Then it has a long E sound. Ali buys a kiwi to put on her ice cream.

I can even be a word by itself.

"I want ice cream," says Iris.

"I will share mine," says Kim.

I makes all kinds of words.

Vowel: I

Which words have a long **I** sound?

Which words have a short **I** sound?

bike

drip

ice cream

sister